MW00654668

THE BLESSED ENTREPRENEUR

5 STEP TO LAUNCH & SCALE A BUSINESS WITH IMPACT

BILLY STICKER

FOREWORD BY MIKE KIM

WALL STREET JOURNAL BEST-SELLING AUTHOR

First Edition

ISBN: 979-8-9863482-1-6

Cover photo credit: Angela Nobles Photography

Contents

Foreword

Purpose. Destiny. Calling. These words have intrigued me for as long as I can remember. They're mystical. They're mysterious. They're also maddening.

Thinking about purpose, destiny, and calling, often leaves you feeling one of two things: you either feel great, or you feel lost.

The problem with obsessing over purpose, destiny, and calling is that there is rarely any middle ground. Our reaction is always one extreme or the other. We seldom give ourselves grace for process, transition, or change.

When I was a teenager, I was heavily involved in my youth group. After graduating college, I served part-time as a youth pastor and then worked full-time as worship pastor at a church in Connecticut.

In my mid-30s, I resigned from that position and spent what seemed like years trying to find myself. Many nights were spent wondering if I flaked out on God's call on my life. Eventually I landed a role as the Chief Marketing Officer of an educational company, and made the leap a few years later to launch my own consulting practice as a brand strategist. This was more than just resigning a few jobs or relocating a few times. The things that once defined me no longer did. That was tough.

I started asking deep, existential questions like, "Am I doing what I was born for? Is my life really making a difference? Did I miss God's calling on my life?"

Here's what I ultimately learned: What you do does not define who you are.

We give too much time, thought, and energy trying to gain affirmation through our occupation. We look for identity in our vocation and when that changes, we freak out.

"Identity" and "assignment" are two very different things. Your work is your "assignment" but it's not who you are. Moreover, there are some assignments you aren't meant to accept.

Let's say I'm an actor, and I hear about a lead role in an upcoming biographical film and plan to audition. You hear me rehearsing my lines:

"I have a dream that my four little children will one day live in a nation where they will not be judged by the color of their skin, but by the content of their character!"

It turns out I'm auditioning for a lead role as Dr. Martin Luther King, Jr. Your mind quickly races to figure out how to tell me, "Um, Mike. You're Korean."

No matter how great an actor I might be, there's no way I'd ever win that role. It doesn't matter if I have better acting ability than Hollywood's leading men; nothing will ever make me ethnically African-American and right for that role.

I will always be Korean regardless of where I live, what I do, or how I dress. I may be culturally different, but when it comes to biology and physiology, that is my identity. It makes that particular acting assignment "out-of-bounds" for me.

Your assignment may change. Your identity in God does not. So, if you're hung up on why something didn't work out for you, or why you didn't get a certain part, please remember not to let that define you.

God never said to me, "You're called to be a worship leader." I have only felt Him say, "You are my child, and for a few years I want you to lead worship."

He never said, "You're a marketer." It sounded more like, "You're my child, and right now you must do this to pay the bills and learn to reflect me among people that don't know me."

He never said, "Your destiny is to be an author! Thus saith the Lord, thou art also a podcaster!"

He just said, "This is the best way you can help people with where I have you in life right now, yet you are and always will be my son. No more, no less." Your assignment can change; your identity in God does not.

Growing up in a Korean church, it was implied that money was bad, and serving God meant you would be poor.

Perhaps it had something to do with Korean culture at the time I was born. My parents grew up at the tail end of the Korean War. They grew up in a survival state of mind rather than one of abundance. This carried over into church and theology. The most noble thing you could do in life is forsake worldly possessions and become a missionary, living off scraps and preaching to the unsaved like John the Baptist. It was implied that if you were really going to serve God, you weren't supposed to have money. It was as if they were mutually exclusive.

When I went to work at the church in Connecticut as worship pastor, things were different. This was predominantly a Caucasian church and was nestled in an affluent part of the country. The members were successful and generous, and the church gave considerable money to missionaries and other causes.

Yet we didn't have a lot of teaching on money other than the importance of tithing and staying out of debt. Dave Ramsey might as well have been the thirteenth disciple. Ultimately, the members were relegated to the three P's: plop themselves into the pew, pray to God, and pay their tithe. That left some of the smartest, most successful people in our community sitting on the sidelines.

In the years since, I've supported various ministries and nonprofit initiatives. Whether it was providing care for a child rescued out of a sex trafficking ring, helping a single parent with their bills, or fixing the roof of a building at a Bible college, I saw many problems that could be fixed simply and quickly with money. Not with prayer, not with fasting, and not with marching seven times around a city and blowing trumpets. With money.

One of the initiatives I founded in recent years is an organization that helps missionaries better communicate with potential donors, raise more money, and get fully funded. I've been hired by some of the world's best-known Christian organizations, as well as some of the leading Christian voices to get Gospel-centered messages out into the business world. While impact can be hard to quantify, my feeling is that I've made a bigger difference when I've had money than when I didn't.

People who have money want to be part of a winning team. They want to give their money towards something that matters, and they don't even necessarily need a return. They just want to know their gift matters. They want to know their life matters beyond plopping, praying, and paying a tithe. There's a world in need, and if money is one of the main currencies we use on this side of heaven, then God's people should know how to earn it, steward it, and give it.

That's what Billy's book is about. I know Billy. I've spent time with him and his wife, and their witness is true. I admire him a lot. The world needs entrepreneurs like him.

As you read this book, you'll realize the world needs entrepreneurs like you. Don't just live for God, live from God. Realize that God's (infinite) resources are available to you, and that one of the great ways we mature and grow is to contribute to those around us. May you make a difference where you are planted in His name, for that is a worthy calling.

Mike Kim
Wall St. Journal Bestselling
Author, You Are the Brand

Introduction

My name is Billy Sticker, and I am both a Christian and the proud owner of a successful business. Sadly, those two things are not always viewed as being in concert with one another, and I'd like to do my part to change that narrative. It is my firm belief that money matters, and I don't believe that concept conflicts with my faith in any way.

The church has done a great job teaching us how to give, but not how to earn. And there is no doubt that giving is an essential part of our faith and what it is that God wants from us here on earth. But there is no giving without earning. What do you have to give if you aren't able to earn?

With this book, I'd like to shine a positive light on earning or making money. Not from a perspective of greed, but from a perspective of providing for our family, our church, and the Kingdom as a whole. Later, I'll introduce you to my P5 Formula for building and scaling a business in the modern digital economy. Before we can get there, however, we need to back up and go over who I am, what I've done, and how I've been brought to the point of sharing this message with you.

PART 1

CHANGING YOUR MINDSET TOWARDS MONEY

CHAPTER 1

MY STORY

I think the story of how I came to the point of writing this book is important to set the stage for everything else I want to share. So, I will try to be concise in this section, while also painting the necessary picture for you to understand what it is I do with my business and what you could accomplish with your own.

Years ago, my life with my wife Rustee looked a lot different. When we were first married, I was working in the oil fields, and later turned to a career in sales. Rustee was going to school for nursing, and would eventually become a home health nurse. We were happy to be living our lives together, to be sure, but we really wanted to be working for ourselves.

In addition to career pursuits, we were also in the ministry for 13 years. Specifically, we were in youth ministry, where I noticed something interesting. I never went to college but knew there were multiple ways to get an education. For me it was books.

I enjoyed reading books about business on various specific topics like sales, marketing, and general success. With those books always in the back of my mind, and doing some work with the youth ministry, I noticed a surprising level of similarity between these two seemingly different parts of my life. Some people wouldn't expect business books to crossover so nicely with the Bible, but that's exactly what I found. I'd read something in a business book and go to my Bible to find scriptures and stories that highlighted the exact same principle.

This couldn't have been a coincidence. The notion that pervades the Church that money is bad and tied to evil just didn't add up to me. The first time money is mentioned in the Bible it's good. (See Gen. 2:11-12)

Money isn't bad. Greed is.

Think about it, who benefits more from us being poor, God or the devil? The devil does. I believe that God is fervently looking for those who will be faithful with their finances that He can download blueprints for business ideas, and the profit from these businesses can be used to further the Kingdom!

Have you ever come away from a lesson in the Church feeling like God doesn't want you to have money? I think that message is often implied, but I think it's off the mark. Rather than saying that God doesn't want you to have money, I think it's more accurate to say that God doesn't want money to have you.

I believe that God doesn't want you to be solely motivated by money and material gains. But that's not the same thing as saying you shouldn't have money, and shouldn't work to obtain more money that can be used for the greater good. It's all about intention and motivation. Are you motivated to earn more money so you can support your family, your community, and God's Kingdom as a whole? If so, I have a hard time seeing how that is not something that would serve the Lord positively. We can do more good with money than without.

A $100,000 Goal

Getting back to the trajectory of my career for a moment and how it led me to this place. When working in sales, I held a commissioned role – I only made money when I made sales. This can be nerve-wracking for some, as it doesn't offer the stability and predictability of a salaried position. At the same time, there is something inherently exciting and motivating about knowing you can make more money if you work harder. This was a great fit for my natural entrepreneurial mindset.

At the time, I was making around $70,000 in commission a year. My next goal was to reach $100,000 a year in income. This seemed like a natural next level to target, and I had written down this goal as well as a few other things I wanted to achieve. What happened next was life changing.

While praying over this list of goals it was like the Holy Spirit stood beside me with His arm around my shoulder and said, "Let's talk about this $100,000 a year income." I immediately started second guessing my goals. I remember specifically saying, "I don't want to be greedy, I want whatever You want for my life."

Then I felt the Holy Spirit challenge me, saying, "What if instead of making that your yearly income goal, what if you made that your goal to give away a year?" I get chills thinking about it to this day. He continued, "I'm looking for people who will commit to that."

Is it possible to give away $100,000 a year? Of course it is. Now the question is who do I have to become to earn enough to give away that much? How many people do I need to serve in business to reach that level of income?

Talk about a huge shift in mindset. Suddenly, I was seeing my relationship with money, and with God, in a new light. It wasn't greedy to earn more and more money, as long as my heart and my intentions were in the right place. If I earned enough to give away $100K a year to better his Kingdom, I would obviously be doing a lot of good in the world – and I would need to earn far more than I had ever imagined.

So, the message I want to pass along from this story of my changing $100,000 goal is this – business doesn't have to be purely about profit. Yes, profits are required to get where you want to go, but you can reframe the purpose of business as ministry. And, with greater resources comes a larger ministry and the ability to impact more people. When seen from this perspective, it becomes easy to find the motivation and purpose you need to get out there and build a business that can serve both your family and your community.

CHAPTER 2

BUSINESS REQUIRES MORE THAN GRACE

How many of us have heard a pastor say something like this, "We gave $XX to the building fund and the next week received an insurance check in the mail we were not even expecting!"? That's grace and grace is good, but God doesn't want to use that to sustain us. He wants to give us ideas that can benefit others and provide for us and our families.

Luke 16:8 reads, in part, that "the people of this world are more shrewd in dealing with their own kind than are the people of the light". Jesus is saying, the "people of the light", or Christians, are not as shrewd in dealing with business matters as non-believers. They are not waiting on grace. They know if they want a successful business they need to serve their clients better than the competition down the street.

As a Christian, we have both. We can have a successful business by serving our clients well. And on top of that God will still give us favor and grace. It's the best of both worlds... literally.

God's Currency is Not Money

So far, what we've been discussing may be challenging the way you have thought about money up until this point – and that's a good thing. As I've said already, the Church is excellent about teaching us to give, and I love that part of our faith. But it doesn't focus on earning, and earning is necessary for giving. You just can't have one without the other, and there is no way around that fact.

Here, however, we are going to get back to an idea with which you are likely more familiar. That is the fact that God's currency is wisdom, not the U.S. dollar or any other denomination from around the world. God doesn't care about the physical money that we pass around between ourselves on a daily basis. What God cares about is wisdom and that you share the wisdom you have found in the Lord with those around you.

The difference in knowledge and wisdom is application. When you have knowledge but don't apply that knowledge to the world around you, the knowledge is wasted. Turning knowledge to wisdom can only occur when you actually put the knowledge into action.

Another key scripture that I like to refer to when discussing matters of business and how it intersects with our faithful lives is Deuteronomy 8:18. It reads "But remember the Lord your God, for it is he who gives you the ability to produce wealth, and so confirms his covenant, which he swore to your ancestors, as it is today."

He gives us the ability to produce wealth. How does He do this? Through ideas and knowledge that we have to apply, which is wisdom.

CHAPTER 3

LOVE GOD.
LOVE PEOPLE.

When asked which of the commandments was the greatest, Jesus said to love God and love people. (Matthew 22:36-39)

Business should be about serving. When we get into the details of my system for creating and running a business later in this book, we will talk about the importance of solving problems in business, and how every business exists to solve a problem in one form or another. With the focus on solving problems, it's easy to see how you can frame running a business as an act of love. After all, what's more loving than helping people solve their problems and live better lives?

Unfortunately, this is often not the vision we have of business. Instead of loving others, we picture business as closed-off board rooms where wealthy people conspire to get even wealthier. Of course, I know enough to know that there certainly is that side of business – but that's not the only way to approach it. Instead, you could approach your business from a perspective of love. You can see everything you do in the business as a way to glorify God and serve His Kingdom to the best of your abilities. Put another way, you can serve God by serving His people through your business.

No one is laying in bed at night thinking of ways to get you their money. People lay in bed at night and wake up in the morning thinking of their problems, their burdens. If you can help them solve their problems they will gladly pay you a fair price for that.

One of my favorite scriptures for connecting my professional, business life to my faithful life is Galatians 6:2 –

> "Carry each other's burdens, and in this way you will fulfill the law of Christ."

I don't think it's a far leap to say that this is a statement about how important it is to help each other solve problems. Rather than leaving people to solve their own problems, you can develop solutions to those problems that are offered through the form of your business. And, in turn, your clients can offer a solution to your problem by paying you for your solutions. These transactions, which we typically think of as just part of our ongoing economy, can just as easily be seen as acts of love.

If you come from a background of earning your living through traditional employment, you have to start to see the world differently when you think about taking the path of an entrepreneur. As an employee, you don't necessarily think much about where your money comes from – your employer just writes a check every couple of weeks, and that's that. They want to pay you, in fact, because you are providing them with your time, hard work, knowledge, and experience.

Once again, no one is sitting around thinking about how to give you their money. In fact, they may not even know you. Rather, they are spending their time thinking about their problems. Think about your own life – when was the last time you sat around and thought about how you could give money to a business? The answer is never. On the other hand, you think regularly about the problems you face in life.

That's how it is going to work for your new business. You aren't going to be overwhelmed by anxious consumers just doing anything they can to hand over their cash. Instead, you'll need to find people who have a specific problem and offer them an appropriate solution to that problem. All along the way, you can see this as an act of love, or service to others.

I'd like to wrap up this section with another scripture, this time from Philippians 2:3-4. "Do nothing out of selfish ambition or vain conceit. Rather, in humility value others above yourselves, not looking to your own interest but each of you to the interests of the others". With that, you have everything you need to focus your energy on starting a business that solves problems.

CHAPTER 4

THE HARD TRUTH – WE ARE NOT EQUAL

In Matthew 25:14-20, Jesus teaches the parable of the talents. The master gave one person 5, another he gave two, and another he gave one. When the master returned, what happened? The one with five talents had doubled his to ten. Most of us have heard this story. The one that had one talent didn't do anything with it because he was afraid.

There are a couple of key takeaways I'd like to point out. One is we are not all equal. For example, I cannot sing. I can't. And that is okay. There are other things I am really good at, like teaching. We are equally valuable, but we don't have the same talents.

That's one point we can take from the story. Another point is he gave everybody a talent. He has blessed you with a gift. You may need to nursher that gift, but God has given everyone some type of talent.

And the last point might be the most important of them all. In the parable, what happened to the one who had the one talent and didn't do anything with it. The master took the talent away and gave it to the one who was faithful with their talents.

We are all equal in the eyes of the Lord. That is something we learn from the Church very early on, and I doubt anyone reading that statement would disagree with it. In fact, that's one of the beautiful things about the Christian faith, and something that we all hold dear. To our Lord, we are all of equal value and worth through Christ.

It's a difficult concept for some to grasp or even discuss, but we are not all equally valuable in terms of the economy here on earth. We all have different gifts, skills, and abilities. However, despite not all having equal value to the economy, we all have talents. Finding your way in business comes down to applying those God-given talents in a way that both serves His glory and solves the problems facing your customers.

Do we all get to earn the same amount of money? No – but that doesn't mean you can't apply the talents you have been blessed with to serve others with those gifts while earning a living for our families and communities.

CHAPTER 5

SELLING IS GOOD

Let's face it – many find selling as an uncomfortable reality of the business world. It would seem, on the surface, to run counter to your faith to aggressively sell products or services that will earn you financial gain.

The first and most important rule of sales: Never sell anything to anyone who wouldn't benefit from it.

Proverbs 11:26 does a great job of highlighting the value of selling. "The people curse him who holds back grain, but a blessing is on the head of him who sells it." Again, it's about solving problems – a theme that is just going to continue throughout the book. It's not shameful or distasteful to sell a solution to a problem. There are thousands of people who need and/or want what you have to offer. Let's say that again... there are thousands of people out there who would benefit from what you have to offer.

In fact, as we've already said, it can be seen as an act of love. Whether it is a grain as in this passage, or anything else that you create that solves a problem for your customer, you are doing good for the world by making that sale.

Proverbs 11:1, "A false balance is an abomination to the Lord, but a just weight is his delight." You are familiar with the justice scales right? The ones where you add weight to one side and it tips the scales. That is what this scripture is referencing. It's about value. Your product, service, or offer should weigh more than their money. That is overdelivering in value.

When people say no to your offer, and it's something they would benefit from, they are saying their money "weighs" more than your offer. Your goal is to stack more value to tip the scales in their favor. When your offer outweighs their money, you have made a sale.

If you focus on value first, rather than money, you'll be off to a great start. Providing value to your customers is an honest, honorable way to approach running a business. It should be the only way to run a business. This is in contrast to simply trying to get as much money as possible out of your customers. That would be a greedy, selfish approach, and not consistent with the virtues we have discussed so far. By flipping that approach around, and asking yourself what you can do to provide as much value as possible for each customer, you will find that you feel good about your sales and good about the role your business plays in the world.

CHAPTER 6

ELISHA AND THE WIDOW'S OIL

Before we wrap up this section of the book and move into my P5 Formula for starting your own business, I want to share one of my favorite stories in the Old Testament. If you would like to read it directly from the scripture for yourself, it can be found in Second Kings 4:1-7:

> "A certain woman of the wives of the sons of the prophets cried out to Elisha, saying, "Your servant my husband is dead, and you know that your servant feared the Lord. And the creditor is coming to take my two sons to be his slaves." So Elisha said to her, "What shall I do for you? Tell me, what do you have in the house?" And she said, "Your maidservant has nothing in

the house but a jar of oil." Then he said, "Go, borrow vessels from everywhere, from all your neighbors – empty vessels; do not gather just a few. And when you have come in, you shall shut the door behind you and your sons; then, pour it into all those vessels, and set aside the full ones."

So she went from him and shut the door behind her and her sons, who brought the vessels to her; and she poured it out. Now it came to pass, when the vessels were full, that she said to her son, "Bring me another vessel". And he said to her, "There is not another vessel." So the oil ceased. Then she came and told the man of God. And he said, "Go, sell the oil and pay your debt; and you and your sons live on the rest.""

There is a lot that can be taken from this powerful passage, but I'd like to focus our attention on three keys –

- The woman sought help. Rather than complaining about the problem, or just accepting her fate, she got counsel and actively worked to find a solution.

- Find someone you are confident can help you accomplish your goals, ideally someone who has already done it for themselves. Agree to pay them whatever price they set and learn from them. This can drastically shortcut your path to success.
  - o In this story, God used what the woman already had available. If you are looking around in your life for a way to make a change and improve your situation, it's possible that God will ask you to simply use what you already have by seeing it in a new way. What are your passions and talents? What comes easy for you? As an example, I knew chiropractic marketing.

- Finally, the solution was to sell her oil for a profit. That was not looked down upon as a greedy or selfish thing to do. It was seen, instead, as the solution to a problem. When selling for a profit in your own business, you can turn to this passage any time you need reassurance that you are doing the right thing.
- Live on the rest. After you meet your obligations, it is okay to enjoy the rest. The problem is many people buy nice houses and cars before being faithful with the first

fruits. This is why they end up with financial problems. It's okay to have nice things as long as these things don't have you. Be responsible to meet your current obligations and tithe first.

PART 2

LAYING OUT THE FORMULA

The P5 Formula

I am excited to dive into the core of this book and go deep on the concepts and ideas that can help you get started on your own entrepreneurial path. I have no illusions of making business easy for you – but it can be simple. The stories I have shared so far in this book should make it clear that I have worked hard and struggled along the way. But the journey has been worth it, and I hope to share what I have learned so that your road to success may be a lot shorter and a whole lot smoother.

The P5 Formula is the framework that I have created for developing a successful business in the 21st century. While we all use the internet on a daily basis for everything from work and entertainment to shopping and communication, only a small portion of the population uses the web to start their own venture. And that's a shame. Simply put, the internet offers a business opportunity unlike any other in history, and getting involved in this market has changed my life.

CHAPTER 7

AN OVERVIEW

The rest of this book is going to be dedicated to a close inspection of each of the five pieces of the P5 Formula. But what are those pieces? Good question –

- Problem
- Product
- Plan
- Proof
- Promotion

That's it. When boiled down to the essence of what it is that has allowed me to find success in business, we are left with those five words. Of course, there are countless details to expand within each of those categories, and I'm excited to share with you everything I've learned along the way.

As you read through the following chapters on each of those five core concepts, you may find yourself wondering if it's too late to get started with an online business. Sure, this all makes sense, but hasn't it all be done already? No! Not even close! When you view the history of the internet in the context of the history of business and industry as a whole, we are just getting started. In fact, you are likely old enough to remember when the internet was just hitting its stride as a mainstream technology. There are a lot of thriving businesses online today, to be sure, but the tip of the iceberg has just now started to peak through the surface of the water. It's still a big ocean out there, and grabbing your share is absolutely possible.

Still not convinced of the size of the opportunity that is resting at your feet? Let's go through a quick exercise to help you truly visualize the scope of what is possible online. While you certainly understand that "a lot" of people use the internet every day, and spend money on the internet every year, it can be hard to grasp just how big of a market is waiting to be tapped.

As a Texan, I'm obligated to reference football at least once in this book – so here it is. At AT&T

Stadium, home of the Dallas Cowboys, roughly 80,000 people gather for a few Sundays each fall to root on their favorite team. It's easy to pass around a number like 80,000 casually, as football stadiums are often near that size, with some even larger in the college ranks. So, when you hear someone say 80,000 people went to a football game, you probably won't even bat an eye.

But I want you to stop and think for a minute about what that means. Imagine yourself walking through that stadium, row by row, to pass all 80,000 of those fans. That's a huge collection of people, and collectively they spend many millions of dollars online each year.

Now, we are just talking about a single football stadium full of people. Naturally, far more than that stadium's worth of fans are going to be shopping for goods and services online. How many more? Roughly 27,000.

That's right – the number of people spending money online during a given year is equivalent to roughly 27,000 football stadiums full of people. I'll spare you the math – that's over 2.1 billion consumers. Do I have your attention now?

It's hard to overestimate the size of the market when doing business online, and the size of the opportunity that is waiting to be explored. Does this massive market mean you are guaranteed to be successful? Absolutely not – but it does mean the right plan and the right attitude could come together with this opportunity to create amazing results.

CHAPTER 8

THE PROBLEM

For me, this is the most exciting part of the book. Of course, I've loved being able to share my story with you, and I hope you have received the message clearly about the size of the opportunity that awaits in the modern digital landscape.

With all of that said, however, I'm all about action. I love getting things done and seeing the results of my hard work come to fruition in the real world. And, it is at this point in the book that we start to get deep into the weeds on how to conceptualize a new business, and how to take that idea and bring it to life.

It is against that backdrop that we get started talking about problems. That's right, problems. Every business – and I mean every single business – is about solving a problem or a set of problems.

If you think of an idea for a new business and you can't identify what problem it is that this potential business solves, immediately toss the idea in the trash. It's only businesses that solve problems that will have any chance of succeeding in the marketplace.

In fact, we can take it a step further – you can define the word "business" as an organization that solves a problem. That is simply what they do. Without problems, there are no businesses. To clarify this concept, look at the following examples –

- A restaurant solves a problem by offering prepared food to customers who are hungry and need something to eat without having to cook it themselves
- An accountant solves a problem by offering financial guidance, preparing taxes, and performing other tasks that individuals are not capable of completing on their own
- A tennis coach solves a problem by teaching students key skills and techniques to improve their techniques
- A roofing contractor solves a problem by repairing or installing roofing materials that meet code restrictions and keep a building dry

- An amusement park solves a problem by alleviating boredom and providing a place for families to play and make great memories

This list could go on and on and on. It would be impossible to list every different type of business and the problems those businesses solve, but you get the idea. Any time you interact with a business, you can quickly determine what type of problem it is that the business solves. Some businesses are laser-focused on solving a single problem. Others are able to tackle many problems with one key product or service. Whatever the case, problems are at the heart of business, and figuring out how to solve them should be your primary concern as an entrepreneur.

One other important point to make on the subject of solving problems – it's important to recognize that these problems will vary in importance and impact. For example, a doctor treating extremely ill patients and a food truck serving tacos are both solving problems. Yes, these are very different problems, and most would agree that treating sick patients is more valuable than serving tacos, but each business model solves a problem and could be a viable venture. In other words, the problems you solve don't have to be life-changing in order to be worth your time and attention. As long as there are enough people who have a given problem, and those people will spend money to solve this problem, your new business could be successful.

The Key to a Successful Business in 3 Sentences

This section does a great job of summing up my ideas of what it takes to be successful.

- If you want to make money, solve problems.
- If you want to make good money, solve expensive problems.
- If you want to make great money, solve expensive problems for rich people (or businesses).

Remember, people will gladly pay you a fair price to help them solve their problems. The bigger and more important the problem, the more you can charge. Ideally you want to do this for people that can afford it, which would include businesses.

Going Back to the Stadium

In the introduction to the P5 system, I talked briefly about the football stadium full of 80,000 people – and how there are 27,000 stadiums worth of people buying things online each year. Let's mentally return to that stadium to talk more about problems and how you figure out what problems to solve with your new business.

As you walk around the stadium, every single person in the building has problems they would like to solve. In fact, they are at the stadium to solve a problem – they wanted to be entertained, and attending a football game was a great solution. Of course, most of these fans have been watching their favorite team for years, so they come back again and again to solve the same problem, which is certainly good news for football team owners. If you can develop a business that solves an ongoing problem, you could find yourself in the same enviable position of serving the same customers or clients over and over again.

So, with so many people in that stadium with problems to solve, how do you know which ones to target? That's a complicated question, and we are going to talk more about it later in this section, but let's start with money. While we certainly want to run our business in service of others, we can't pretend that money doesn't matter. It does, and the more of it we make, the greater the impact we can have in the Kingdom. Solving problems for the wealthy people in that stadium offers potential rewards that are not available if you serve the greater population.

- With that in mind, it's pretty easy to understand which problems we want to solve – it's those that are worth the most to the customers and clients we serve. The more value we can provide, meaning the bigger the problem we can solve, the greater the rewards will be. There are two general ways in which we can create the opportunity to make a lot of money with this venture –
- You can solve a small problem for a large number of people. These problems aren't worth a lot, so you'll get a little money from each customer, and you'll need to do a lot of volume to make it add up at the end of the month

You can solve expensive problems for wealthy people. There are fewer of these problems, and there are fewer potential customers who fall into the "wealthy" category. Only a small number of customers is needed with this type of business, but they can be harder to find

It is my strong recommendation to focus on solving expensive problems for wealthy people. In fact, you could make that the mantra that guides your new business –

"Solve Expensive Problems for Rich People".

Make note that you can solve these kinds of problems on either a personal or professional level. So, your new business could solve expensive problems for business owners, who tend to be wealthier than those who are employees. Or, you could serve wealthy people on a personal level, solving problems that they have outside of work. Either way, big-ticket products and services that focus on a small number of customers or clients are the way to go.

Three Keys to Solving Problems

The concept of solving a problem is simple enough. You solve problems for yourself all day, every day. When you wake up in the morning and feel thirsty, you head to the kitchen to find a glass of water or cup of coffee. Life is an ongoing string of solving problems, so much so that doing it is largely second nature.

However, solving problems for other people is a bit different. You can solve your own problems however you see fit, but you'll need to present solutions to other people and businesses in a way that convinces them of your value. Here are three things you'll need to reliably and consistently solve problems for others –

- Passionate goal. It all starts with a passionate goal. If there is no target for what you are doing – a goal, in other words – you'll never know where you are headed. And, if you don't have passion for reaching that goal, you won't have the motivation needed every morning to get started and put in the hard work. Nothing about succeeding in business is easy, even when you have a great plan, so it's essential to have passion for reaching your goals. I should point out that your passion doesn't need to be pointed in the direction of the specific problem you are solving. Rather, your passion can simply be regarding how you will create a successful business that supports your family and allows you to serve God's Kingdom. As an example, do you think business owners in the janitorial space wake up each morning feeling passionate about cleaning floors and rinsing toilets? I doubt it. What they are passionate about, however, is building a thriving business – and solving the problem of dirty homes and businesses is simply a means to an end. If you feel passionate about creating a life-changing business, that is more than enough motivation to carry you through the tough days.

- Proven plan. The proven plan you bring to your business is the roadmap for how you will actually solve the problem you promise to solve with your products or services. We will get into this idea in greater detail below with an example from my own business, but it's important to have this in place as soon as possible. It's one thing to tell someone that you can solve their problem – it's another thing entirely to have a proven method for getting the job done. With a proven plan in place, you won't be all talk. Instead, you'll have proof that you know how to solve a given problem, and potential customers will have a reason to believe that you can repeat your process and apply it to their situation.

A big part of developing and deploying your new business is going to come down to how well you can build a proven plan that will serve customers who have the desire and means to pay for that solution.

- Purposeful confidence. The confidence you have to deliver a solution is tied closely to the quality of the plan that we discussed in the previous point. If your plan is good – and you know it – you'll naturally be confident in your purpose and direction with the business. False confidence doesn't serve anyone's needs. Rather, it's the authentic, legitimate confidence that stems from knowing you have effectively solved a pain point that will allow you to grow in the months and years to come. As your plan falls into place, you will feel the confidence grow within you and you'll be excited to share it with the world.

At this point, I'd like to bring these concepts to life by walking you through my experience in starting a business that serves chiropractic offices. I believe my story can be inspiring to those who are anxious to start their own business but are plagued with self-doubt regarding their abilities – or more importantly, their qualifications – to make it happen.

As far as qualifications to handle marketing for a chiropractor, I had none. Well, at least, none of the traditional qualifications that you would see on a resume. I don't have a degree in marketing. I was not a long-time employee in the marketing space, with several notable campaigns or accomplishments to my name. In fact, in the years leading up to this new venture, I had been selling rare coins. That's right – rare coins. I'm not sure you could get much farther away from chiropractic marketing than being a rare coin seller, but that was the transition I managed to make. So, how did it happen? It went like this –

- I was making good money in my sales role, but I didn't enjoy the business and wanted to do something else.
- There was a chiropractor operating two locations that was looking for marketing help. Despite my lack of formal training, I had confidence in my ability to get the job done based on the countless books I had read on related subjects.

- When I contacted the chiropractor, Dr. Scott Kerr, regarding this job, I submitted not only a resume – but an eleven page marketing plan as well. It was essential that I demonstrated how I was going to accomplish the goals for the practice. In other words, I was presenting a plan – one which was not yet proven, however.

- After interviewing around 10 people, and after conducting three interviews with me, I got the job. The difference-maker was the marketing plan I put together that showed Dr. Kerr exactly how we were going to accomplish his goals.

This is a nice story, but what does it have to do with you starting a business? After all, you are looking to strike out on your own, not land a new job. That's where the story gets even better.

In less than a year after starting this job, volume in both of the practice locations had doubled. And what does that mean? That's right – my plan was now proven. The critical piece of the puzzle that we discussed earlier was now in place because my ideas had been put to the test and were proven in the real world.

Do you think other chiropractors would like to learn what we were doing to double the size of both offices? Absolutely!

With a proven plan on my hands, I began to teach other chiropractic offices what I had learned, and what started as a regular job turned into a growing business.

A Look in the Mirror

Let's turn our attention away from my story and towards your future. It's easy to find inspiration in successful business stories, whether it is my own or any of the many others you can find scattered across the web. But how do you translate those success stories into actual progress on your own venture? You probably aren't going to start a chiropractic marketing agency like I did, and you probably aren't starting out as a salesman for a rare coins dealer.

So, where to start? There are three places you might find the seed of what could someday grow into a thriving venture –

- Expertise. If you are already an expert in something, this is an excellent way to get started. If you already have expertise you are a step ahead of the game. Be sure not to discount any expertise you have in a certain area because you think people don't need that kind of problem solved. With nearly any expertise, there will be a way to spin it or adjust it to match up with a problem that people are willing to pay to solve. In this way, the exact idea for your business might not present itself right away. I have heard that to become an expert you only need to read the top five books on a subject. That will put you far and above most. In the planning stage, simply write down any area that you would consider yourself an expert, or close to an expert. Later, you can think about what type of product or service you might be able to develop in that space in order to turn your existing knowledge into a profitable business.

- Experience. While expertise and experience are often closely connected, they are not the same thing. Look into your past and think about how you have spent your time. This will often mean looking at prior work experience, but it could also be personal experiences from your private life that wind up paying off in a professional context. Experience is a valuable asset and not enough people take advantage of the experiences they have when trying to start a new business or get a new job. Don't let all the time and energy you have spent in the past go to waste by tossing that experience out the window and turning in a completely different direction. And, just as we discussed above with expertise, you might not immediately know how you are going to apply this experience to a new business, and that's okay. Just document what experiences you have in life and start to sort through that list until an opportunity becomes evident.

- Passion. Finally, you may want to turn to one of your passions for inspiration as you seek a direction as an entrepreneur. Earlier, I talked about how you don't have to be passionate about the subject matter of your business by using the example of a janitorial company. That's true, but it doesn't mean you have to run away from your passions, either. If there is something you simply love in life and you want to spend as much time as possible around that thing, consider angling towards that for your business. It may even be possible to create a business around your passion if you don't have any expertise or experience in the space just yet. If that is true, do your best to connect with current experts and prominent people in the field to gradually grow your own profile and create a base of knowledge. My ChiroCandy Podcast was an excellent way for me to interview some of the top people in that industry, and this built my authority and grew my agency as a result.

In the real world, your path to a new business probably won't be as cut and dried as simply looking in one of these three categories for the right idea. More likely, you'll have some blend of these points that helps you focus your attention on something that allows you to solve important problems for people who can pay for solutions.

A Thorough Examination

As we wind down the Problem section of this book, we need to ask one key question that should be near the top of your mind as you go through this process –

"Is it a business?"

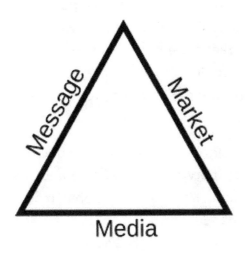

Put another way, you need to constantly be considering whether or not the idea you have developed in the back of your head has everything it requires to actually come together as a business. Solving a problem is the key component, as we have been discussing, but there's more to it than that. Dan Kennedy likes to explain that there are three things required for a business to exist – a market, a message, and a media. All three of these elements are essential, and missing just one is going to leave you without a business that has any chance to succeed. I love this framework, so let's look at it a little closer.

First, the market. This is what we have been talking about repeatedly so far, going back to the football stadium full of people with problems. A viable market for a business is one that contains enough people with both a given problem and the means and desire to pay for a solution to that problem.

On this point, it's important to understand the connection between market size and the cost of the problem. Imagine a fictional market where you only can land one customer per year? Is that a viable business? Before you say no, you need to understand how much the solution to that problem is worth to your single customer. If that customer would pay $1 million to make the problem go away, you certainly would have a business – even with just a single customer.

Of course, if your one customer is only willing to pay $10 to solve the problem, you don't have a business at all. At that price point, you'd need a hundred thousand customers to make the same million dollars in annual revenue. Solving a problem that is only worth $10 to your customers means you need a huge customer base – and likely plenty of recurring purchases – to build a business.

So, on the point of establishing a market, you need to consider both volume and value. A viable market can be a small group of wealthy people willing to pay large sums for your solution, or it can be a huge group of average people willing to pay modestly. Or it can be somewhere in between those two extremes. If you can't qualify a market that makes sense based on the problems you are proposing to solve, there is no business to be had.

If you are able to determine that a market is available, your next step is creating a message. The message is the process of explaining what it is that you offer and how you are going to solve a particular problem. This is essential, and it is easily overlooked. If you have developed a solution to a problem, whatever that problem may be, the solution is obvious to you – because you developed it. But, when taking it to someone else to make a sale, it will be anything but obvious. As a result, you might find people who would legitimately benefit from your solution not being interested in making a purchase, simply because they don't understand it. Only when you can craft a message that is properly received will you be able to properly convey the value that you are presenting.

As you craft your messaging, remember that simplicity is the name of the game. Your goal is to fully explain what it is you offer in as few words as possible. You want to avoid overwhelming your target audience with information. A great filter question to ask is would a 5th grader understand? There will be time later to get into the details for those customers or clients who want to know more – at the start, you are just trying to get the point across without saying too much or losing their interest.

This brings us to the third and final element, which is the media that you will use to deliver this message. It's likely that you will use the internet to connect with your audience, but even that isn't specific enough to know how you'll get the point across. Are you going to use written content on your website? Display ads on other websites? Video content on platforms like YouTube? The possibilities are endless, and plenty of different methods can work effectively. Before you know you'll have a business on your hands, you have to make sure that you can identify an effective medium to find your market and deliver your message.

We have covered a lot of ground in this discussion on how problems are at the heart of all businesses. With any luck, your wheels are already turning with ideas on problems that you can solve and what the market might look like for those solutions. Next, we are going to turn our attention to the actual product that you will sell.

CHAPTER 9

THE PRODUCT

To start a business, you need to have something to sell. That might be the most obvious point I make in the whole book, but it still needs to be said. All the ideas in the world are never going to make you a dime if you don't distill them down into something that you can exchange for money that your customers or clients are willing to spend.

So, it is against that backdrop that we turn our attention to the product that will act as the foundation of your business. As a point of clarification, I'm using the word "product" as a simplification – what you are selling could be just about anything, including a physical product, consulting service, digital course, and on and on. It's easier to say "product", but know that I'm using that word to represent the whole universe of things that you may choose to sell.

If you have read through the book in order to this point, you already understand that your product needs to solve a problem. That's the whole point – identifying a problem and finding a way to solve it. Solving the problem of a customer's hunger could be accomplished with a cheeseburger, a taco, or any number of countless other food items.

An Entrepreneur – Not an Inventor

There is an old saying in business that you may have heard before. It goes something like this –

"You just need to build a better mousetrap."

What does that mean? The idea here is that you don't have to invent an entirely new product to succeed in business. In other words, there have been many mousetraps made over the years, and new designs and ideas for the same product are continually being brought to the market. Some people get stuck in a pattern of thinking that they need to create something entirely new from scratch to find success in business, and that just isn't the case.

With that said, you aren't going to want to simply copy a product being sold by someone else and call it your own. That's not a winning strategy, and it could land you in legal trouble. Rather, the idea here is to build on what is already selling in the real world, only making it better or changing it in some way to perfectly solve a problem for a specific set of people.

Let's go through an example to bring this concept to life. When Apple presented the iPod to the market, it was not the first small, portable device to play MP3 files. It was, however, with little argument, the best in its category. So, Apple didn't invent something new out of thin air, but rather it saw the growing popularity of this category of product and set out to make the best one in the world.

The story is the same with the iPhone. Was the iPhone the first smartphone option for consumers to purchase? No, but it took that product category to a higher level and became the most prominent player in the space in short order. Even if you operate on a far smaller scale than Apple or other tech giants – and we all do – you can still learn from this example and approach your product development process in the same way.

How My Product Came to Life

It's hard to relate to the giants of modern industry like Apple, but you can certainly relate to my story of going from an employee for a rare coins dealer to the owner of a successful chiropractic marketing agency. I'm just like you, and as the old cliché goes, if I can do it, you can do it. So, let's walk through how it was that my product development process played out many years ago.

As we have already covered, I didn't enter the marketing space with a degree or strong background behind me. Rather, I learned from countless books, came up with my own ideas, and put together a plan. That plan was good enough to earn me a job in this space, and I was able to then prove that my plan was a winner based on the results it yielded for my employer. That's a great start, but it's certainly not a business – it's still a job.

The turning point was when I realized that the same problems I was solving for the chiropractor who hired me were sure to be experienced by chiropractors all over the country. Certainly, this wasn't the only chiropractic practice struggling to bring in new patients, and many of those chiropractors could benefit from the same techniques and strategies that I was deploying in my job. If there was a "light bulb" moment for me in this whole process, that was it. I knew deep down that this was a problem I could solve for many other chiropractors, and now it was just a matter of making it happen.

Think about the problem you serve at your current job. Would other companies benefit from what you do? Could you turn your knowledge into a consulting business? I know an attorney that was on staff at a large organization for many years. She talked with the powers that be and now that same company is her client, not her boss. She is now free to work with other organizations while working for herself, not an employer.

Fortunately, at the same time, I was learning about internet marketing. Don't be put off by the terminology "internet marketing" – there is nothing fancy or overwhelming here. It's simply marketing, any form of marketing, that is performed over the web. You encounter internet marketing every day when you use the web, whether you know it or not. Those ads you see on social media? Internet marketing. The blog posts you read that are filled with specifically chosen keywords to draw your attention? Again, internet marketing.

As I was learning more and more about internet marketing and how it can open up a business to a massive market, I started to see how my experience and growing knowledge in marketing chiropractic offices could be leveraged through this means. Think back to the discussion of needing a "media" from the previous chapter. I already knew the market and I had the message, and the realization was quick to follow that internet marketing was going to be my media. This is how I would form the connections I needed with many chiropractors across the country to turn my marketing plan into a full-fledged business.

Bringing this new vision to reality was not glamorous, but it was effective. It went something like this –

- The year was roughly 2008, and I decided to create a product that would share my knowledge and marketing ideas with chiropractors. So, I headed to my bedroom with my laptop and a USB headset, and I recorded a training course. This was me laying out exactly how I was successfully marketing the chiropractic office where I was employed, and offering advice on how other chiropractors could do the same.

- Since technology was not nearly what it is today, I took the content I created and had it burned on CDs. That's right, CDs. You probably haven't seen one of those in a while, but that's how I started to distribute my message. In fact, I had six CDs created and I took them to eBay to see if I could sell one. Somewhat to my surprise, there were plenty of bidders on the auction, and the CD sold for nearly $70. Instantly, I had strong proof of both my concept and my market. Not only did I sell that CD to the winner of the auction, but I reached out to the bidders who didn't win and was able to make sales to some of those people, as well.

- Not only did that content, which was called Profit Practice, sell in CD form on eBay, but I also had it transcribed and turned into an eBook which was sold on Amazon. Of course, the price for a book, as opposed to media content, was lower, but it sold nicely for years and helped countless businesses improve their marketing processes.

- Then, seeing that these books could sell and were a great way of distributing a message to an audience, I started to think that chiropractors themselves might like to create books to explain what they are all about. So, my next course went through the details of how to create a book, including details like interior design, cover design, content writing, and much more.

There are a couple of important things that I want you to take away from this journey. First, I didn't start out with anything particularly fancy or polished. I didn't have a lot of equipment, a producer, or anything else. It was just me, my laptop, and a headset. I was simply trying to find a way to share the knowledge I had with people who could use that knowledge to solve a problem. And therein lies the beauty of this kind of business. Knowledge is something that doesn't run out, and you don't have to order more inventory to keep it in stock. You record it once and sell it over and over.

You find a way to share what you know and you find other people who can benefit from that information. It's easy to overcomplicate the path to a successful business, but it really can be that simple. Get out of your own way, stop thinking you need to do something that changes the entire world, and just share what you know with the right audience.

The other important takeaway here is to note how my product offerings quickly changed as new ideas revealed themselves along the way. In the beginning, I didn't even know if this was a business – so I listed a CD on eBay to see what would happen. When that resonated with my audience, I started to find new ways to connect with these people, through eBooks and courses that taught my system. Suddenly, it wasn't just one thing I was selling, but a few different things, and the evolution has continued from there.

Start a Business, Not a Job

Throughout this book, we have been talking about what it takes to start your own business. There is something deeply appealing about owning and operating your own business, and I'd like to think by the time you reach the end of this book that the dream of being a business owner will be closer than ever before.

With that said, you need to be careful that you don't accidentally create a new job for yourself, rather than a business. It's easy to fall into this trap. While it might look like you are a business owner from the outside, the reality could be that you simply work for a business that you happen to own. This is an important distinction and something you should keep in mind throughout the planning and development process. One good question to ask yourself constantly is as follows –

"How will I gradually take myself out of this business as it grows?"

The only way to scale a business is to build it so that it can grow without you doing all the work. You'll never have more than 24 hours to use in any given day, and you can only do so much. And, the whole point of building your business is to buy yourself the freedom to do the other things that are important to you in life.

I like to use the example of the dentist and the roofer to illustrate how important it is to think about this concept when going into business. Imagine the case of a dentist who opens her own practice, serving patients in a small office. Most people would consider that to be a "business", and by the traditional definition, it is. However, this dentist is only going to make money when she is actively serving patients – working, in other words. When no treatment is being performed, no money is being made. That's not to say that dentists can't earn a good living, because they certainly can, but a dentist operating a solo practice will forever be actively working for all the money they make - that is a job.

Next, let's talk about the roofer. On the surface, you would probably imagine dental work to be more lucrative than roofing. After all, one is a profession that requires years of study and training, while the other is a job that may be obtained almost immediately out of high school with no higher education. Roofing is certainly not easy – there is a lot to know and learn – but it doesn't come with the same barrier to entry as something like offering dental care.

Despite that, I have a friend who decided to go into business as a roofer with not even a bit of experience. He approached it as a business venture pure and simple, seeing a large potential market and an opportunity to grow. He laid the groundwork by doing research and educating himself on the industry, and opened up to start serving clients – while using crews to do the actual work. So, while making good money in the roofing industry, my friend very rarely finds himself up on a roof. Rather than building a job for himself to work in, he built a business that he can run while others do the work.

I want to make it a point here to say that you aren't going to be able to remove yourself from the business on day one. Take the example of my own business, ChiroCandy Marketing. At the start, it was me doing everything from top to bottom. I certainly couldn't afford to hire help at that time, since the revenues of the business didn't warrant that kind of expense. However, as the ball started rolling and the bottom line started to add up, I could gradually pull myself away and let others implement what it was that I had put in place.

It is this outsourcing of implementation that is the ultimate key to scaling your business up. If it's only ever you that implements the ideas and strategies of the business, scaling will be nothing more than a dream. However, if you can make the transition – gradually, over time – to have others doing more of the work for you, there will be no limit to what you can accomplish.

The Many Plans

To wrap up this section of the book, I want to quickly highlight a few basic business plans that you may want to consider. Before I do that, it's important to note that your chosen strategy should be a result of the problem you want to solve. Find the problem that you are going to solve first, then select the best plan to arrive at that solution for your customers and clients. If you go through the process backward, you may find yourself trying to use a plan that doesn't really fit the problem that is being solved. I'll say it again for effect – business is nothing more than solving problems. Find the problem first, then set about devising the right way to solve it.

- Software as a service. Don't run in the other direction simply because the word "software" appears in this idea. You don't have to write a single line of code to create a piece of software, and using software is a great way to solve problems. Once you have identified a problem that exists in a certain market – say, for real estate agents – you can get to work on figuring out how a new piece of software can effectively solve that problem. Then, contractors can be hired to do the work of bringing your idea to life. Once you have guided them towards the finish line of a piece of functional software that eases a pain point, you can sell the software as a one-off purchase of a monthly subscription.
- Digital marketing agency. This is the model at Chiro Candy, and it's a good one. The key here is to get specific with the types of problems you are going to solve and who

you are going to solve them for. It's not good enough to say that your marketing agency is going to help businesses get more customers. That's too generic and it doesn't speak to any particular business owner directly. We have been able to find success with our agency because we specialize in chiropractic and we've been laser-focused from the start on helping practices find new customers using our proven methods. If you have experience in a particular market and you understand the pain points in that space, consider using that as a starting point to develop a marketing plan that can earn you your first clients.

- Consulting. There is a lot to like about the consulting model, but it can be dangerous in that you might find yourself with a job rather than a business. If the plan is simply to apply your own knowledge and experience in a given space and share that insight with clients, you'll have a job in no time at all. So, from the start you need to be thinking about how to systematize the operation, using your knowledge to create processes and plans that clients can use to get where they want to go. This is also easy to scale from one-to-one consulting to one-to-many, creating time leverage.

To be sure, these three points only scratch the surface of the many different methods you can use to solve problems for your customers. Keep an open mind as you get started, and don't eliminate any potential plan until you have identified the one or two that seem to be the best fit for your upstart business.

CHAPTER 10

THE PLAN

With a problem identified and a product developed, your next step on this journey is assembling a plan that will bring everything together. It's painfully easy to just get started without any specific plan for how you are going to connect with your market and make sales, but rushing into action in this way is sure to fall short. As the saying goes, "if you fail to plan, you plan to fail."

Fortunately, a solid business plan doesn't have to be a long, complicated, drawn-out document. It can be pretty simple – and, in fact, it probably should be pretty simple. The plan that you use to get your business started should focus on simplicity and actionable steps. You can't plan out every last detail, because you don't yet know what is going to happen once you start your business. You don't know what you don't know, in other words. Instead of aiming for the details with your business plan, sketch out the big picture of how this business will work and then set about creating systems that bring it to life in a sustainable way.

Planning a Lifestyle

When you hear the words "business plan", your mind immediately jumps to visions of charts, graphs, and other relatively boring documents. And I'm not going to argue that you don't need any of those types of strategic documents, because they can be very helpful in starting and running a business. But that is not where we are going to start in this section.

Instead, we are going to be talking about how you plan a lifestyle and built a business that supports the lifestyle you have envisioned. After all, we want to create a business that is going to serve your life, not a life that is going to serve your business. If you are going to do the things you want with your limited time on this planet, and if you are going to have the freedom and resources to serve the God's Kingdom, you are going to need to design this new business very carefully from day one.

Now, it's important to remember that what is an ideal lifestyle for one person may not be appealing to another. So, with the bullet points below, I am going to touch on some of the biggest keys for me and my family as we planned out the lifestyle we wanted our business to support. This list could look different for you, although I imagine the priorities I had in mind will be shared by many others who are seeking an entrepreneurial lifestyle.

- Working from home. This was a requirement – I didn't want to be tied to a physical location to do my work. With the digital agency, I am able to work from anywhere I have a computer and an internet connection. More and more, people are seeking this kind of flexibility in their work, and it really is as good as advertised. If you have been working in a specific physical location for your entire career, you won't believe the freedom that you feel when you suddenly realize that your new business can be run from anywhere. Even if your business can't be run entirely remote, I suggest you make it as location-independent as possible based on your niche, so you can enjoy the freedom that so many others have started to experience.
- Own your schedule. Another one of the pain points for the average employee is lacking

the freedom to set their schedule and decide when they do what it is they want to do. Over the years, I've had many conversations about the travels I enjoy with my family and how we are able to make it work while running a business. Whether it was London, Paris, Italy, or any other thrilling destination, we have been fortunate to see much of the best of what the world has to offer. Without a business that put my lifestyle first, none of this would be possible.

- Shape your day. The way you spend your days is the way you spend your life. So, make sure the content of your days lines up with what you want out of this world. For me, that means avoiding client calls when at all possible. I simply don't want to sit on calls hour after hour, day after day – that just doesn't get me excited for life. Don't get me wrong, I'm passionate about delivering excellent results for my clients, but I don't think those results come as a result of ongoing calls. So, the business has been designed to minimize the number of calls I need to take. And, I've set limits on when those calls can take place. As a starting point, I simply do not take calls on Mondays or Fridays, and certainly not on the weekends. So, already, we are down to Tuesday – Thursday for possible calls, and even then, I've put restrictions in place. On those three days, I don't take any calls prior to 10 a.m., as I value my time in the morning to go to the gym, have some food and coffee, and get the day started properly. I like to wake up when I'm done sleeping, not to an alarm clock.

You might find that what you read about doesn't sound much like the "hustle, hustle, hustle" culture that seems to pervade modern entrepreneurial endeavors. And that's true. I'm not interested in the hustle lifestyle – I'm interested in an enjoyable lifestyle that blends work with plenty of relaxation, hobbies, travel, and more. Building your business so it serves your whole life is the opposite of just hustling every working hour of the day. And not only is this approach more enjoyable, it's also more sustainable over the long run.

As you go through the process of lifestyle planning and figuring out how your new business is going to facilitate the lifestyle you desire, be sure to go into as much detail as possible. Thinking about these points can be helpful –

- When do you want to get up? Yes, this is the level of detail I'm talking about when planning out how your future will look. For me, I don't want to be controlled by an alarm clock five days every week. Instead, I want to get up when I'm done sleeping, like I mentioned earlier. That's a simple concept that is surprisingly rare in the modern world. Many people are forced to get up when the alarm clock says so, and for me, that's not an enjoyable way to live. Some days I'm up and running at 7 o'clock – on other days, it's not until after 8. So, that's an important piece of flexibility to me, and as a result, I prioritize the ability to start my day slowly when designing how my business will work.
- Travel. I mentioned this earlier, by my family loves to travel. It is a big part of our lives, and we value the flexibility offered by our business. Not everyone places the kind of premium on travel that we do, so think about this for yourself and consider how much time you'd want to have available during the year to take trips.
- Do you like working with people? If you are going to scale a business, you are almost certainly going to need to work with at

least a few other people. But not everyone wants to build a huge team with people all over the world that need to be managed and supported. While I've been able to scale up a successful business that doesn't rely solely on my labor, I actually don't like to manage a big, distributed team. I try to keep my people relatively local, and I manage the size of the team so that we can keep up with demand without being too big for our own good.

Going Fishing

With all the talk about leisure in this section of the book, you might think I'm talking about literally going fishing here – but that's not the case. Instead, we are turning our attention to the part of the plan where you determine how you are going to find clients. Remember back to my story, I actually got started on eBay of all places, selling my training CD through an auction. That's probably not going to be your plan, but there are plenty of other alternatives that are likely to be far more effective.

As a starting point, before you go out and look for these clients, you'll need to get inside their heads and understand what they are looking for. Yet again, this comes back to understanding their problems. Think carefully about what it would be like to be in the shoes of your ideal customer, and vividly imagine how they might be thinking about their problems currently. You have a process in place for solving that problem, but you need to find these people and convince them that your solution is the right one.

When you feel like you have a firm grasp on what it is your target audience is looking for and how they are thinking about their problems, it will be time to actually go find these people. For now, one method for doing just that is Facebook ads. Nearly everyone is on Facebook, whether for personal or professional reasons. And one of the best things about running Facebook ads is the ability to drill down your campaign based on demographics and other factors. So, if you have a clear vision of who your clients are, you can focus your campaigns on targeting those people and save money by not showing ads to those who are unlikely to be interested.

With regard to running ads to find clients, I have some good and bad news. First, the bad news – there is a learning curve with paid ads. You'll need to do plenty of experimentation with things like bid amounts, platforms, ad copy, and more before you dial in a formula that works. With that said, the good news is that online ads are easy to test for only a modest investment. You don't have to spend thousands of dollars to put your ads to the test. Instead, you can spend modestly, a little at a time, while tweaking your ads and testing the results. Only when you are confident that you have landed on a winning ad will you want to up the investment and turn up the speed of client acquisition for your business.

We All Need a Coach

A popular way to approach online business these days is to offer coaching services. This is basically the modern equivalent of traditional consulting services. And, to be sure, there is a lot to like about coaching. However, I have concerns about the model of one-on-one coaching services, as there are only so many hours in the day. It's going to be hard to make enough money during the available hours in the day if you only coach one client at a time. And, even if you do make enough money to satisfy your needs and meet your goals, you'll find that you are working too much, and you may shortly burn out on the whole endeavor.

Group coaching, when managed properly, is a much better model. The reason I like group coaching is due to the way it can leverage your time for higher returns. Sure, you are still spending that time coaching, but instead of offering knowledge and advice to just one paying client, you are doing so for several clients at the same time. Even if you have to offer a slightly lower rate per client due to the group setting, you'll still make more in total than you could ever make with the one-on-one approach.

Also, I believe there are benefits to group coaching for the clients, as well. When in a group setting, clients are able to get to know others in their field, who are trying to solve the same problems. This can enable them to build a powerful network that can be used for support and even for business opportunities. Others in the group coaching session may have questions that spark new ideas, or the overall discussion may bring something to mind that simply had not been considered previously. However it plays out, there is a lot to like about group coaching, and I recommend those with something to teach at least consider this model as one of their offerings.

So, what is the right product or service for you to sell? I certainly can't say from my position, but I think you are getting closer and closer to being able to make that decision confidently for yourself. As you continue to read through this book, you'll hopefully gain even more clarity on what you can offer and how that offering will solve problems for the clients you have in mind.

CHAPTER 11

THE PROOF

It's possible – and maybe even likely – that the proof stage of my P5 Formula is going to be the most difficult for you to tackle. This stage is challenging simply because this is where you need to get out into the real world and prove that your solution to a given problem is a winner. You'll need to do this for two reasons. First, you have to prove to yourself that this solution works – the confidence you gain from proving it to yourself will be massively helpful as you try to make sales.

And, of course, proving it is going to make selling your solution far more viable. It's one thing to tell a prospective client that you have a good solution for their problems. It's another thing entirely to actually demonstrate how that solution has worked in the real world. You'll find that the demonstration is much more effective in closing deals than anything else you can bring to the table.

Every Situation is Different

The first thing I want to make clear about proving your product and your solution to someone's problems is this – the right proof is entirely dependent on what you are trying to sell. Let's take some examples to see how this works –

- If you are selling marketing services for a certain type of business, you'll want to prove that your methods have helped previous clients generate new business. That could come in the form of raw data from some of your past clients, testimonials directly from the mouths of those clients, etc.

- If you are selling a fitness program, you'd want to demonstrate the before and after fitness levels of previous people who have used your methods. This could again come in the form of testimonials, but it could also be some simple photographs that you have permission to use.

- When selling software as a service, you could demonstrate the various ways a business could benefit from using your software, such as specifics on time saved on certain tasks, money saved by eliminating errors, and more.

There is no one-size-fits-all here, but as we'll see as we work through this section, a couple of themes keep coming up again and again. Let's move into a story from the development of my agency to highlight how opportunities to create proof can arise virtually out of thin air.

Taking on a New Challenge – and Opening Doors

A few years back, we were working with one of our chiropractic clients write a book. At some point along the way, the client asked about the possibility of getting some help with his Facebook ads. While they had been trying to run ads on Facebook, the results were disappointing – the leads weren't rolling in and the account even got shut down at one point.

So, knowing we offered expertise in marketing for chiropractors and knowing that we had been doing good work on other marketing fronts, this client hoped that we could take the reins and get his Facebook ads campaign on track. There was only one problem – this wasn't a service that we offered to our clients at that time. Sure, we had run some Facebook ads of our own, but we didn't do it for clients and had to give it a shot on the fly when given the opportunity.

What happened next was a big step forward for our business. We got to work on the Facebook ads for this chiropractor and brought in 50 leads during just the first month. He was thrilled with this result and we had strengthened a relationship with one of our clients. But what happened as a side effect was even more important – we had established proof of real-world results for our ability to run Facebook ad campaigns. Quickly, this doctor began to refer others to us for the same work, because he was so impressed by what we accomplished. Suddenly, somewhere around 10 accounts were paying for Facebook ads management, which was a service we didn't even offer a few months before.

The point of this story isn't that you need to immediately dive into Facebook ads. Rather, the important takeaway here is that you can seize opportunities when they come up and potentially walk away with that valuable proof that can be so difficult to produce otherwise. If we had tried to sell Facebook ads management services cold with no proof, it never would have happened. But the circumstances that came up – with a client who already trusted us and needed some help – were ideal for expanding what we could offer.

Another Form of Proof

The classic form of proof for a business product or service is to show how well it has worked in the real world. And, most likely, that is the most powerful thing you can put in front of your audience. With that said, there is another form of proof that will go a long way toward establishing yourself in a market, and that is the legitimacy that comes from becoming a known entity in a particular niche.

I'll give you an example from my experience growing ChiroCandy. Right from the start, I had the Chiro Candy podcast, and the presence of that show went a long way towards making me known in the space. Even if someone knows nothing else about you or about your business, the fact that you are active enough in the market to host a podcast says a lot about your investment in finding success for your clients. It's not likely you would go through the trouble of launching and running a podcast if you weren't in this market for the long haul.

So, how can this notoriety turn into powerful growth for your business? It all comes down to making connections and building relationships. At one point, I had the pleasure of interviewing a man named Dr. Eric on my podcast. Not only was he well-connected in the chiropractic world, he also held an event where many top doctors from around the country would be in attendance. Based on the strength of our conversation and his knowledge of how my agency was serving clients, he asked me to speak at that event.

My talk was on Facebook marketing for chiropractors. Not only was I able to offer some practical advice, but I was also able to promote my services and I had special offers available for new clients who signed up right there at the event. When my speaking time was up, I headed back to my booth and waited anxiously to see if the message had connected with many of the doctors in the audience.

As it turns out, it had. One new signup turned into two, and pretty soon there was a line forming in front of the booth. Roughly 20 new clients signed up for services right then and there, and my business was transformed overnight. My first phone call was to my wife to tell her it was time to quit her job and get on board helping me run this rapidly expanding business. I still get chills of excitement thinking back to this event and the role it played in getting us to where we are today.

All of this came from the social proof associated with hosting a podcast and having the opportunity to interview interesting guests. I would have struggled – and probably had no chance at all – to grab Dr. Eric's attention if it wasn't for my podcast. Through that medium, I landed a chance to speak in front of many chiropractors anxious to grow their business, and in turn, my own business grew by leaps and bounds.

Testimonial Truth

As you use the web on a day-to-day basis for your own personal and professional reasons, you are sure to see testimonials and reviews everywhere. And, as you can probably guess, these are popular for a reason – they work. Hearing directly from a past customer or client about how a business was able to solve their problems goes a long way toward convincing future customers that they should make a purchase. Simply put, testimonials are a powerful resource, and you should absolutely find ways to put them to use in your business.

So, that's the end of this section, right? Not so fast. While I love testimonials, it is important to make sure they are implemented in the right way in order for them to be effective. If you don't put much time or thought into how you'll present these testimonials to your audience, they might come up short of your expectations.

The standard playbook for businesses who want to use testimonials is to ask past customers or clients for a quote that they can put on their website. Then, while building out a page on their website – likely a landing page used to sell products or capture name, emails and possibly phone numbers – the business will include a section of testimonials attributed to these various clients. There are a few issues I have with this approach –

- Visitors to your site might not read them. Virtually every business website has a testimonials section, so it would be easy for someone to gloss over this part of your page. They have seen this before, and most testimonials say pretty much the same thing, so why bother stopping to read?
- They could appear fake. Even if your testimonials are 100% legitimate, your site visitors might not believe what they are reading. After all, we know that you can't trust everything you read on the web, so how can they be sure that these testimonials are actually coming from your clients and are

not just copy that you wrote and added to the page?

- They lack emotion. This is perhaps the biggest issue I have with standard testimonial content. With the written word, it's hard to properly convey the emotion associated with having one of your problems solved. So, even if your clients are extremely satisfied with what you have delivered, their satisfaction might not come through so forcefully in a written testimonial. Instead, it might feel more like they are saying "yeah, they did a good job." Which, while technically an endorsement, it's exactly the kind of thing that will make people rush to buy from you.

If written testimonials suffer from some of these issues, you might be able to guess what the solution is going to be – video testimonials. Where written content comes up short in this area, video won't let you down. First, it's much easier to get visitors to engage with video content than written content, given the popularity of video on the web today. So, present them with a section of video testimonials and you'll be likely to get plenty of views on those recordings. And, it's easier to track engagement with these kinds of testimonials as opposed to the written version, since you can simply see how many times any video has been watched.

Next, it's much harder to fake a testimonial when you capture it on camera. Sure, you could technically hire someone to pretend to be someone else and read off a script, but that would be a long way to go for a marginal gain. Most likely, people are going to trust the video testimonial content they see, and you can even add an element of social proof by asking the person giving the testimonial to state who they are and who they represent.

Lastly, and clearly most important, you'll get all the emotion you need through video as compared to written content. When the person in the video talks about how your business was able to solve their problem, the emotion on their face will make it clear that you have done great work. They don't need to be crying or anything like that – just the authentic emotion that comes with telling a story about how your business served their needs is going to connect with a big portion of your audience.

I'll be the first to admit that collecting video testimonials is more work than asking for a quick written quote. With that said, I'm firm in my belief that it is worth the extra effort to get this kind of content from your customers. Virtually everyone has video equipment capable of capturing a testimonial, whether by using their smartphone or the camera on their computer. To make this as easy as possible, create a short template that they can follow while recording, helping them to organize their thoughts and present their experience clearly. With just a bit of editing after the video is submitted to clean it up and cut out any unnecessary time, you'll have a powerful marketing asset that you can display in a number of locations both on your site and on social channels.

Simple Math

It's easy to make sales more complicated than it needs to be. At the core of the matter, selling anything is all about providing value to your customers. We've talked extensively about how business is all about solving problems, and that remains true, but each one of those problems you solve has a value attached to it. If you solve a cheap problem but ask for $5,000 in return, you aren't going to make any sales – even though you technically are solving a problem.

When selling to businesses, the simple math you need to do is confirm that the money you are asking for is less than the value of what you are offering to the client. The math is easier here than when selling to consumers because businesses only deal in dollars and cents – it's black and white. Either they expect to come out ahead or they don't. So, if you can present a strong case that proves working with you will be worth more to them than it will cost, making the sale will be a foregone conclusion.

This is the final piece of the proof puzzle. Finding the right way to prove that working with you is going to be a net positive for the bottom line. If the client hands over $5,000 to invest in your product, and you can demonstrate to them that the investment of $5,000 will lead to $10,000 in revenue, they will sign up as fast as you can put the offer in front of them.

CHAPTER 12

THE PROMOTION

Now that you have worked your way through the other P's down through proof, it's time to promote. This is where you really begin to grow and scale your business. For some Believers, promotion can be difficult. In fact, while building proof for your business is certainly a big challenge, some may find this last piece of the P5 puzzle to be even more difficult. After all, we learn through the Church that we are to be humble in service of the Lord, and promotion feels like the opposite of humility.

So, our first challenge here is to overcome this mindset and change the way we approach promotion. It's not about telling the world how great you are or why they should ignore the competition and turn to you instead. Rather, we are going to again come back to the idea of solving problems for the right perspective on promotion. You are simply trying to help someone else solve a problem with your business. When framed that way, helping another solve a problem suddenly sounds like exactly the kind of thing you like to do as a Christian... serve.

Craft Your Message

Before you spend a single moment thinking about where you are going to present your message to your target audience, I want you to first spend as much time and effort as necessary to perfectly craft what that message will be. You already understand that you need to have a solution to someone's problem in order to have a business, but that's only half the battle. The other half can be found in explaining to a potential customer that you have that solution and that it is worth their money to purchase the solution from you.

There is an art to be found in crafting a sales message, and you could certainly read book after book on this topic. However, you can get started without reading a library full of books if you just follow the general outline I've provided below. As you review this outline, think about your own business idea and how your problem/solution combination could be presented in a way that would make for a compelling offer.

- Meet them where they are. You want to enter the conversation your potential clients are already having in their minds. One of the key tenets in sales psychology is meeting your customer or client wherever they currently are in their journey. In other words, you want to make it clear that you fully understand what they are going through, the problem they are facing, and how they need a solution to that problem right away. Do your best to use this message to connect with your audience on an authentic level. Of course, due to that, you need to truly understand the depth of the problem you are solving and why it's a problem in the first place. Let's use a simplified example from the restaurant world to bring this concept to life. On the surface, a restaurant simply sells food. So, when crafting their messaging to the target audience, they should just talk about the food they sell – right? Not even close. If you pay attention to restaurant marketing you encounter, whether it's a TV ad or an online promotion, you'll find they actually talk very little about the food. It will be touched on, of course, but it's actually the other benefits offered by the restaurant that are highlighted in marketing efforts. For a fast food restaurant, the focus is often on how much time you can save by picking up dinner instead of cooking it yourself. So, they aren't keying on food with the messaging, but rather on time savings. Alternatively, a high-end restaurant might focus on the relaxing, comfortable experience you'll have by sitting down for a nice meal while a babysitter watches the kids. Again, it's not about the food so much as the experience and what it brings into your life. This is a valuable lesson even if you don't have any intentions of selling food. Craft your message based on the underlying problem that you'll be solving, rather than just the problem on the surface. Get to know the industry and the people within it, and truly understand their pain points... what keeps them up at night? Then, and only then, will you be able to create a message that rings true with your target audience.

- Boil it down. Here's a common problem found by business owners who get into the process of crafting their marketing message – they wind up with a list of selling points, features, and benefits that runs off one page and onto another. Simply put, you aren't going to have enough time in front of a prospective customer or client to present that much information. It has to be boiled down as far as possible, so that only the core essence of what you are selling remains. This can be a big challenge, to be sure. As you work on it, keep saying two words to yourself over and over again – problem and solution. What's the problem that the potential customer is facing, and what solution are you offering? Those are the two core elements that need to be featured in the message, and you'll want to get those across as quickly as possible. People pay for results, not products. An incredible example of this kind of messaging comes from Snickers candy bars. Without me even telling you, it's likely that you'll know the marketing slogan used for Snickers – "Snickers Satisfies". From a marketing perspective, that is beautiful in its simplicity. They managed to present both the problem and the solution in just two words! It's hard to imagine it could be done any faster than that. Compare those three words to something like this – "If you are hungry after a long day at work or out exploring the town, consider a Snickers bar as a quick and delicious way to get.....". You get the idea. Most people would stop reading such a message long before they finished it. All that flowery language is simply not needed, and it gets in the way of the core message. You might not be able to achieve the same accomplishment of capturing your entire message in two words, but aim to be as concise and memorable as possible while bringing your message together.

- Create a personality. Consistency in your brand's messaging is important, and one good way to create cohesion from promotion to promotion is to have an identity that guides your style. For example, you could decide that your messaging is all going to have a confident, almost confrontational tone. Some brands have had success with that approach. For others, it works better to be a little bit funny or even sarcastic. Or, you might want to play it safe and use messaging that is fairly generic in its tone and doesn't risk ruffling any feathers. Whatever the case, try to establish this tone early on and keep it consistent over the years. This will also help if you wind up having more than one person work on your marketing materials. With a style guide in place that explains the preferred tone for all customer-facing messaging, you'll maintain cohesion even as your company grows.

- Customize based on medium. As your marketing efforts grow and expand along with your business, you are likely to explore more and more avenues for advertising opportunities. With that in mind, remember that your messaging will need to be adapted to suit all of those various mediums. When using paid ads on Facebook or another platform, you'll have to be short and to the point. Your ad won't get much screen space. This is where it's particularly important to boil down your message as I mentioned earlier. On the other hand, if you use a video platform like YouTube to get your message out, you might have more space to expand on your selling points. Creating a marketing video that you load to your own YouTube channel – so it's not technically an ad – will give you all the time you want to dive into the details of your product offerings and how you can solve a customer's problems. Continue to adapt and adjust your approach to messaging based on the platforms that you employ.

It should be clear by now that you'll have plenty of work to do when crafting your marketing message. This is likely to be one of the areas where you spend the most time, and there should be some trial and error involved to dial in this message just right. Keep the four keys listed above close at hand throughout the messaging process to make sure you stay on track.

Be Discoverable

The web is a huge place. In fact, it's hard for a single human being to get his or her head around how big the internet truly is. While we all interact with this modern digital tool on a daily basis, the fact is most of us only scratch the surface of what's available online. It is estimated that nearly 5 billion people on the planet use the internet in one form or another. That's a scale that's hard to understand while stuck inside a human brain.

Needless to say, you can't advertise your new business in every far-reaching corner of the internet. However, you do want to carve out a sizable footprint to make sure you can be discovered in a variety of ways. If you stick with only one or even two forms of marketing online, you'll be missing out on a huge portion of your potential audience by failing to meet those customers where they spend their time.

Given the scope of the internet and the bountiful opportunities in front of you, it would be easy to get lost in the weeds. You could find yourself stuck in planning mode, never actually getting any marketing off the ground because you are overwhelmed by the choices. Don't let that become your reality. To help you avoid that fate, I'm going to offer some pointed advice in the list below.

- Pick one starting point. Yes – there are tons of ways to promote a business online, and yes, you should consider exploring many of them in the months and years to come. But you shouldn't be doing them all at once when you get started. Instead, just pick one that you feel comfortable with and get going right away. So, for example, you might decide to dive into Facebook ads as a starting point. With that decision made, you can get to work on learning as much as possible about how ads work on Facebook and how you can make them work for your business. Set aside a small amount of money for your first run of ads, work on your messaging, and see how they do. Most likely, your first effort won't be a home run, but it will be a starting point and you can go from there. Once you get a little traction on Facebook ads, or wherever you decide to start, you can move on from there to options like YouTube ads or videos, Google ads, TikTok, and on and on. And, as you gain experience, you'll find that what you learn on one platform often applies to the next, so all of these campaigns will build on one another and your process will continue to improve.

- Consider a book. I'll be honest – I love the marketing power of a book for countless types of businesses. Writing a book brings instant authority or author-ity. There is something about the way you can connect with an audience through a book that just isn't possible with any other form of promotion. When someone commits to reading a book that you have produced – which will be given away for free, in most cases – they are committing to learning about your brand and your products. That's a big commitment, and it takes you much closer to closing a deal. Don't be overwhelmed by the prospect of taking on this project, as it's easy to get help with every step along the way. You don't even have to write a single sentence to have a book created that can be used to bring customers along on a journey. A book project is a good thing to take on separately from learning how to run ads, since it is such a completely different method of customer acquisition. By working with a good freelance writer, and a designer who can polish up the finished product, you can have a book to distribute in either digital or physical form after only a few short weeks in many cases. If there is a story you want to tell that never quite seems to fit within the compact spaces on online ad copy or even within a video, use a book to give that idea room to breathe and spell everything out for your interested audience. Unfortunately, roughly 90% will not read the book. It still serves as a fancy business card that will generate business.

- Build a funnel. This is a key point that is missed by many people who are starting their first business. If you are just getting going with your marketing efforts, you might find that you are doing a good job of getting attention – yet you aren't doing much with that attention that you gather. In other words, you aren't converting your new leads into actual paying customers. Building a funnel can be rather complex, but the idea is pretty straightforward – you craft a system that is meant to take people or businesses from the start to finish in their buying journey. So, the start is when they first come into contact with your brand, and the finish is when they commit to spending money with you. Often, a prospect won't be ready to buy immediately, even if they like your message and would be willing to pay for a solution to their problem. So, the funnel can do the work of taking them along the way and working toward that ideal outcome. You'll never convert 100% of your prospects into buyers – not even close – but a good funnel can capture as much revenue as possible from the leads you manage to acquire. While it's understandable to keep costs as low as possible in the early days of your business, paying to get help building out a great funnel might be an investment that is worthwhile.

Eventually, you want to spread out wide and cover as much of the internet's real estate as possible – at least, the portion of the web that is relevant to your business and what you offer. Trying to do that right from the start, however, is a recipe for trouble. You are going to find that it's overwhelming to take on too many marketing channels at one time, so get focused and prioritize masterful execution above all else.

Two Key Metrics

Throughout the rest of this book, you may have noticed that we have been largely staying away from complex business concepts, metrics, and anything else that might be intimidating for someone just getting started. And, of course, this is on purpose – you don't have to have those things mastered to get started with a new business. You'll learn as you go, and you will find important ways to measure and track how your business is performing once it gets off the ground and makes a few sales. These are called Key Performance Indicators (or KPI's).

In this quick section, however, we are going to break with that trend and talk quickly about an important metric that you will want to start tracking as soon as you get going with any kind of paid marketing. The good news is this metric is very easy to understand, and relatively easy to track, even for a beginner. The metrics I want you to learn are these – Lifetime Value of a Client and Cost of Customer Acquisition.

As you might be able to determine from the title of this statistic, you are going to use this to measure how much it costs you to acquire a new customer for your business. It's important to note that this is not the same thing as acquiring a new lead. A lead is someone who may eventually turn into a customer, not someone who is already a customer. So, with this stat, you'll be keeping track of how much money you spend compared to how many new customers come into your business. A quick example is in order to make sure we are on the same page –

- Imagine you get started with a Facebook ads campaign to reach out and find new clients for an agency you have started. With your first run of ads, you decide to spend $500, and that amount of spend allows you to keep the ads active for a week.
- After a week goes by, you review the results and find that you have booked two new clients from those Facebook ads. You may have been contacted by several leads who saw your ads, but only two decided to sign on the dotted line and work with you.

- The math is quite simple – you divide the $500 in ad spend by the two new clients you were able to book. In this case, your cost of customer acquisition would be $250.

Knowing what it cost to get a new customer into your business, the next question is obvious – "Is that good?" There is no magical number that is "good" or "bad" for customer acquisition, as it depends entirely on what kind of business you run and how much you charge for your services. For a coffee stand selling drinks for under $5, a $250 customer acquisition cost would likely be a disaster. On the other hand, a business selling high-ticket consulting services would love to book each new client for only $250.

When I said I wanted to introduce you to one business metric, that wasn't quite accurate, because there is one more than is needed in this equation. That is the estimated lifetime value of a new customer or client. This is another simple one, but it can be a little harder to calculate, at least in the early days. The point here is to determine how much the average customer will spend with you over the lifetime of their engagement with your brand. By comparing that number to how much you have to spend to bring in each new customer, you can figure out whether the cost of a certain method of advertising is a wise investment in the end.

To wrap up this discussion, let me share with you some numbers from my business to further bring the conversation to light. For us, a new client is worth at least $10,000, and potentially much more. So, it stands to reason that we are able to spend significantly for our leads and customers, because there is so much to gain when a customer is added to our list. Paying as much as $3,000 to get someone on a call is still a logical move to make, since we know from experience that somewhere around 70% of our scheduled calls eventually turn into active accounts. Even if the cost of customer acquisition hovering around $5,000, we'd still be in great shape in terms of a return on our ad spend. Fortunately our acquisition cost is less then $500.

A Different Form of Promotion

As we wind down our discussion on promotion, I want to turn the direction of that word a little bit. So far, we've been talking about promotion in the advertising sense – you put your business and your products in front of potential customers using a variety of platforms. That's a critical piece for any business, but it's not the only kind of promotion that matters. Just the same, you need to be actively promoting people to play the roles they were meant to play in your business.

At the start, it's likely that you will be playing all of the roles. Need to create the actual products that you sell to your customers? It's on you. Require marketing materials to distribute your message to the market? Again, that's your job. Have to update the website, pay some bills, or answer customer support questions? You, you, and still you.

This is fine in the beginning, but it is not sustainable and won't lead you anywhere you want to go. Delegation is inevitable for a successful business, yet it can be hard for entrepreneurs to let go of control. Often, the person who started the business feels like he or she is the only person who can do the work the right way. But that's usually not the case. With some training and a little practice, you can probably delegate many of the mundane tasks on your plate to someone who can do them just as well, if not better.

One of the experiences that changed the way I look at business and helped me create a better business as a result, was an event I attended that included a session with a man named Dr. Pete Camiolo. This is the exact formula I used to scale ChiroCandy to over $3million with me working as little as 10 hours per month. The points below are going to roughly outline the message he delivered –

- He presented his ideas using the metaphor of a typical stoplight, where there are three different colors used – red, yellow, and green.
- 1. Our first task in this session was to take a moment to write out everything involved in our business that we simply don't like to do. These are the tasks that come up day after day that seem to drain time out of the schedule without moving the needle in any notable way. 2. The next step was to write out all the things that we don't really mind doing, and we know how to do them well – but they aren't particularly exciting at the same time. 3. Finally, and you can see where this is going, we were asked to write down the tasks that we felt highly motivated to take on within the business. Often, these are the things that are going to lead directly to sales or will allow you to deliver great service for your customers.
- Each of those three lists of tasks – which should now represent most of what has to get done to keep your business running –

is assigned to a color on the stoplight. The tasks you hate doing go into the red-light column. The things that are just okay are put into the yellow light column. Lastly, those jobs that you love to handle are given a green light designation.

- The takeaway from this exercise was this – those things that fall in the red-light column, immediately be delegated to someone else. Never do them again. The yellow light items are things that you may continue doing for a while but should probably aim to outsource at some point because they aren't your main focus or priority. And, of course, the green light jobs are where you should spend the vast majority of your time, not only because you enjoy them, but also because they will allow you to have the greatest impact on the future of the business.

This concept had a profound impact on me and how I chose to run my business. It helped me let go of certain operational aspects and hand them over to other people. That's a hard thing for an entrepreneur to do, but it was unquestionably the right thing, and our business would not be where it is today without letting go of some of that control. And, once you get used to the feeling of letting other people take on some of the responsibilities in the business, you'll find that those people have their own strengths to bring to the table, and the organization as a whole will be better for their contributions.

What's Next?

I can't properly explain the excitement I get from sharing my story with you in this book, and from providing the P5 outline that I believe can help you launch a successful, fulfilling business. Not only is there excitement to be found in the financial rewards that may be waiting, but also in the opportunity you will have to build God's Kingdom through your accomplishments.

For a moment, however, I do need to temper that excitement with some real-world advice. After reading a book like this, which I hope has been full of inspiration and has caused you to think of your own ideas, you will be ready to hit the ground running. Your motivation will be at an all-time high, and you just can't wait to get out there and conquer the world.

And then, reality smacks you in the face. You see, the trouble is that building a business doesn't happen overnight, and it is easy to feel overwhelmed by the process once you actually get started. Things feel great in the "dream phase", while all of this is still something you are imagining could happen one day. When you start to bring it to life, however, things might not feel as good and you will encounter plenty of roadblocks along the way. Many potential entrepreneurs have struck out with the best of intentions – and great ideas – only to get frustrated and overwhelmed and give up before they really get started.

I don't want that to happen to you. So, my last piece of advice as we wrap up this book is that you will need to be stubborn about building your business. Once you have identified the problem you are going to solve, and once you have created a plan to solve that problem, be stubborn about making this thing a reality. It's going to be hard, there are going to be setbacks, and you are going to get frustrated. Don't let those obstacles defeat you. Keep your ultimate goal of building a thriving business and serving the Lord at the front of your mind and draw on those visions for inspiration when the days feel difficult.

Fast-Track Your Success

One of the best things you can do is hire a business coach. Find someone who has accomplished what you are wanting to do and pay them whatever their fee is. This can easily be your fastest and cheapest path to success.

So, what's next? Get started. Just get started. Your first action toward starting a new business doesn't need to be dramatic, and it doesn't need to be impressive. It could be something as simple as taking out a piece of paper and creating a list of potential business ideas. That's a first step. It's a long way from a thriving six- or seven-figure business, but every journey starts with a single step.

Make a huge list with every potential idea that you may want to consider, and then start working through that list one entry at a time over the days to come. Which ideas deserve more consideration, and which can you quickly cross off because they don't fit what we've discussed in this book. You now have more knowledge about starting a business than you did just a few days ago, so you'll be able to make confident choices about how to proceed.

I have been blessed to enjoy such a wonderful journey with my business, and my hope is that you will be able to experience many of the same blessings. And, as you start to find financial success and build a business that is on firm footing, I trust that you will use your opportunities and resources to continue to glorify the word of God and expand his Kingdom here on earth.

Be Blessed,

Billy

About The Author

Billy Sticker is a speaker and business advisor who helps business coaches, consultants, agency owners, and authors who want to launch and scale a multiple 6-to-7 figure business. He is the author of several titles, including Tribe of Patients: Building an Audience of Quality Practice Members in Your Market.

He is a multiple winner of the coveted Two-Comma Club Award presented by ClickFunnels, recognizing entrepreneurs who have generated over $1M in revenue through online sales. He is also the winner of the Multiple 7-Figure Agency award for his company, ChiroCandy, given to entrepreneurs who have built a multiple seven-figure agency.

Billy has been interviewed on industry-leadings podcasts including Internet Business Mastery, Seven-Figure Agency, and The Christian Entrepreneur. Billy has also been featured in Forbes, Inc. Magazine, ABC, CBS, and Fox, and has spoken at global industry events across the USA, London, and Paris.

Bonus Content

join the Blessed Entrepreneur Facebook™ group for kingdom minded agency owners, coaches & course creators...

Inside, You'll Get Access To...

Weekly training classes on how we're generating multiple **7-figures per year** in our coaching business working as little as 5 hours per week...

Multiple value posts each week outlining mindset shifts **& marketing strategies** we're discovering in our own business...

 AND SO MUCH MORE...

You can join by going to:
blessedentrepreneur.com/group

CPSIA information can be obtained
at www.ICGtesting.com
Printed in the USA
BVHW081232130722
641604BV00007B/21